Conservation of Mass

Jenna Winterberg

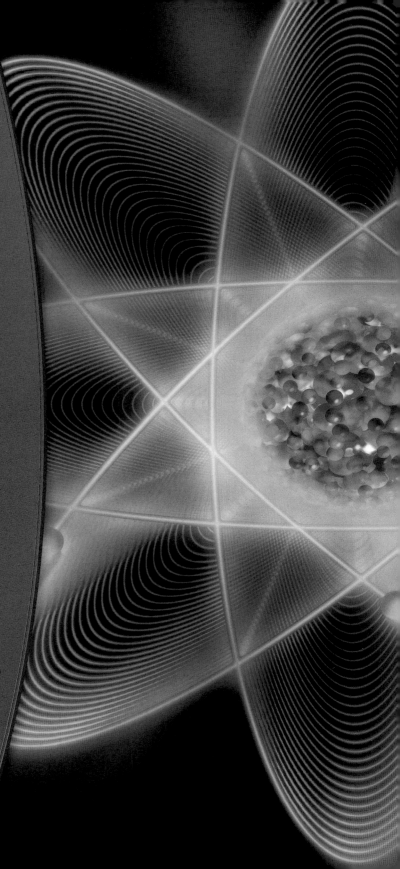

Consultant

Brent Tanner
Mechanical Engineer

Publishing Credits

Rachelle Cracchiolo, M.S.Ed., *Publisher*
Conni Medina, M.A.Ed., *Managing Editor*
Diana Kenney, M.A.Ed., NBCT, *Content Director*
Dona Herweck Rice, *Series Developer*
Robin Erickson, *Multimedia Designer*
Timothy Bradley, *Illustrator*

Image Credits: p.2 Mike Agliolo/Science Source;
p.4 Science Photo Library/Alamy; p.6 iStock; p.7
ESA/NASA/SOHO; p.8-9 iStock; p.10 Charles D.
Winters/Science Source; p.13 Photo Researchers,
Inc.; p.15-16 iStock p.16-17 (background) iStock,
(molecule) SPL/ Science Source; p.17-18 iStock;
p.19 Bill Sanderson/Science Source; p.20-21
Science Source; p.22 Martyn F. Chillmaid/Science
Source; p.23 © Pictorial Press Ltd/Alamy; p.24
Royal Astronomical Society/Science Source; p.25
© National Geographic Image Collection/Alamy;
p.28-29 (illustrations) Timothy Bradley; p.31-32
iStock; all other images from Shutterstock.

Library of Congress Cataloging-in-Publication Data

Winterberg, Jenna, author.
  Conservation of mass / Jenna Winterberg.
    pages cm
  Summary: "You can't make something out of nothing.
This is because there are certain laws that everything in
the universe follows, including the conservation of mass.
It may seem like magic, but it's really a matter of matter"--
Provided by publisher.
  Audience: Grades 4 to 6
  Includes index.
  ISBN 978-1-4807-4722-7 (pbk.)
 1. Mass (Physics)--Juvenile literature.
 2. Relativity (Physics)--Juvenile literature. I. Title.
  QC173.36.W56 2016
  530.11--dc23
                            2015002710

Teacher Created Materials
5301 Oceanus Drive
Huntington Beach, CA 92649-1030
http://www.tcmpub.com
ISBN 978-1-4807-4722-7

Table of Contents

Something Out of Nothing

It's lunchtime, and you're absolutely starving. You think back longingly to the packed lunch you left behind in your refrigerator this morning. Then, you count the spare change in your pocket—not quite enough to purchase a cafeteria lunch. Your parents are at work, and your friends have nothing to spare. So, with no other options, you pull a meal out of thin air.

If only you were a wizard! In reality, we can't wish something into existence. You can't turn nothing into something. You also can't turn something into nothing. Take that broken object you desperately want to hide from your mother, for example. You can sweep it under the rug, but you simply can't make it disappear.

What's the Matter?

Atoms, the smallest bits of matter, make up everything around us. It's rare to find atoms alone. Instead, they bond with other atoms, creating **molecules**— groups of two or more atoms.

Matter is the same way. Matter can neither be created nor destroyed. Matter is all that stuff that makes up the universe—solids, liquids, and gases. It's the air we breathe, the clothing we wear, and even our bodies. If it isn't there, we can't create it. And if it is there, we can't get rid of it. It's the law— more specifically, the law of conservation of mass.

The most important law for modern chemistry is the law of conservation of mass.

The law of conservation of mass is sometimes called the *law of conservation of matter*. Mass measures how much matter something contains. The first part of the law—that we can't create mass or matter—is self-explanatory. That's what would make magic lamps so special: It would take a genie to make things appear out of thin air.

The second part—that we can't destroy matter—is more complex. Let's say you've written a secret on a piece of paper. To prevent it from being read, you could rip it up into tiny little bits. It would certainly be harder to read. But all those tiny parts could be put back together. The same amount of paper is still there, just in pieces instead of as a whole.

So, what if you were to toss the secret paper into the fireplace the next time your parents lit it instead? Now, chances are the paper would burn to ashes. Your secret would be safe. You wouldn't be able to put the note back together, after all. Nonetheless, you'd still have the same amount of matter.

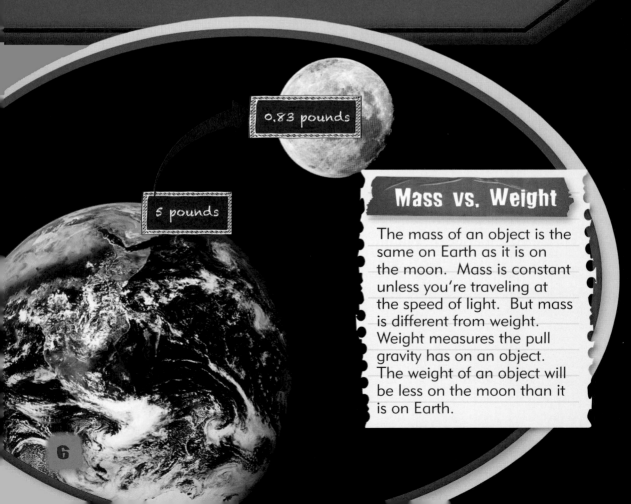

0.83 pounds

5 pounds

Mass vs. Weight

The mass of an object is the same on Earth as it is on the moon. Mass is constant unless you're traveling at the speed of light. But mass is different from weight. Weight measures the pull gravity has on an object. The weight of an object will be less on the moon than it is on Earth.

Don't Forget Plasma!

Although you see solids, liquids, and gases every day, you shouldn't forget about the fourth state of matter—plasma! Plasma is mostly found in stars. It is a substance similar to a gas but it has extremely high temperatures and can carry electricity.

Although plasma is uncommon on Earth, it makes up 99 percent of visible matter in the universe.

Physical Changes

Ripping up the paper is an example of a **physical change**. A physical change affects the way something looks—such as its size, shape, or color. Its appearance has changed, but its makeup is the same. Crumple paper, break glass, or juice an orange. The items will look different, but your actions won't create something new or different. The change is physical. The object's chemistry is not altered.

Sometimes, mixing things will result in a physical change. Mix cinnamon with sugar. The two become hard to separate, but no new substance is created. This is an example of a mixture.

Now, add sugar to water. The sugar will dissolve into the water, making a solution. But the **properties** of the sugar and the water haven't changed. The makeup of each substance is the same as before. The change is physical.

Changes in states of matter are also physical changes. The solid, liquid, or gas state doesn't alter the properties of the substance. When water turns to ice, it's still water. Freezing the water doesn't change its chemistry.

Changing States

Seal three ice cubes in a zipper bag and weigh them. Then, let them sit in the bag and melt. Weigh the bag again. There will be no change because the mass of water is always the same, no matter its state.

Same Chemistry

Here are a few ways to make a physical change:

- heating
- boiling
- drying
- crushing
- mixing
- evaporating
- freezing
- separating
- distilling

Chemical Changes

Just as with physical changes, **chemical changes** can alter the way things look. But in this case, it isn't just size, shape, or color that differs. A chemical change affects the very makeup of something.

A chemical change results in something new. This new thing is a **product**. It's different from the original substance, or the **reactant**. The new product can seem a lot like the original item. A boiled egg still resembles a raw egg. Yet it's the product of a chemical reaction. Cooking changed the chemical properties of the egg. When apples decay, they turn into vinegar. This is a chemical change. There are similarities between the apples and the vinegar. But each substance has its own unique makeup.

Spot a Change

It may be difficult to observe a chemical change. But look out for these signs:

- bubbling/fizzing
- color change
- smoke
- heat
- light

Old Fruit

When you cut a piece of fruit open and leave it out for a few days, it starts to turn brown. If you let it sit for long enough, it will even start to grow mold. Both are chemical reactions.

The new product can also seem quite different. Think back to the burned paper. The fire changed the paper into ash. Not only did it look different, it *is* different at a molecular level. Its chemical makeup has changed.

All of these products are different at the molecular level. In other words, the molecules have a new setup. The basic building blocks of the substance have changed.

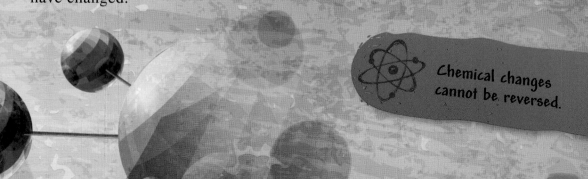

Chemical changes cannot be reversed.

With a physical change, we can measure the volume or weight of the item before and after the change. It would be easy to show that the amount of matter was unchanged.

With a chemical change, the matter can take a new form. For example, the volume and the weight of the ash will not be the same as the paper before it burned. Still, the law of conservation of mass tells us that no matter was lost. So what happened?

A fireplace is no place to conduct a scientific experiment. Ash falls in many directions. Smoke escapes through the chimney. Nothing is contained or controlled. If we could burn paper in a sealed container, we could contain our experiment. It's impossible to do, but let's pretend we can. The paper and the oxygen in the jar would create the products of water vapor, carbon dioxide, and ashes when burned. The ashes wouldn't have the same mass as the original piece of paper. But the products have the same mass as the paper and the oxygen. No matter is lost—it is simply changed.

If you could light a fire in a sealed jar, it would not burn for long. Fire needs oxygen for fuel.

Observing Evidence

Does this picture show a physical or a chemical change? Write a list of words to describe what you see.

Systems

Mass is always conserved within a system, or group of parts that work together. There are many types of systems. A system may be as tiny as a cell or as large as the universe. A fish tank is a system. A forest is a system. A cell phone is a system. When studying how mass is conserved within a system, it is important to define the system's parts. Then, you can study the parts separately. It can be hard to study a system without its environment getting in the way.

The best way to see how mass is conserved is to isolate a system. This means to look at it apart from its environment. This way, nothing can escape, like the smoke that escapes through the chimney. Let's consider how mass is conserved in a very tiny system.

The solar system includes the sun and all the objects that orbit it.

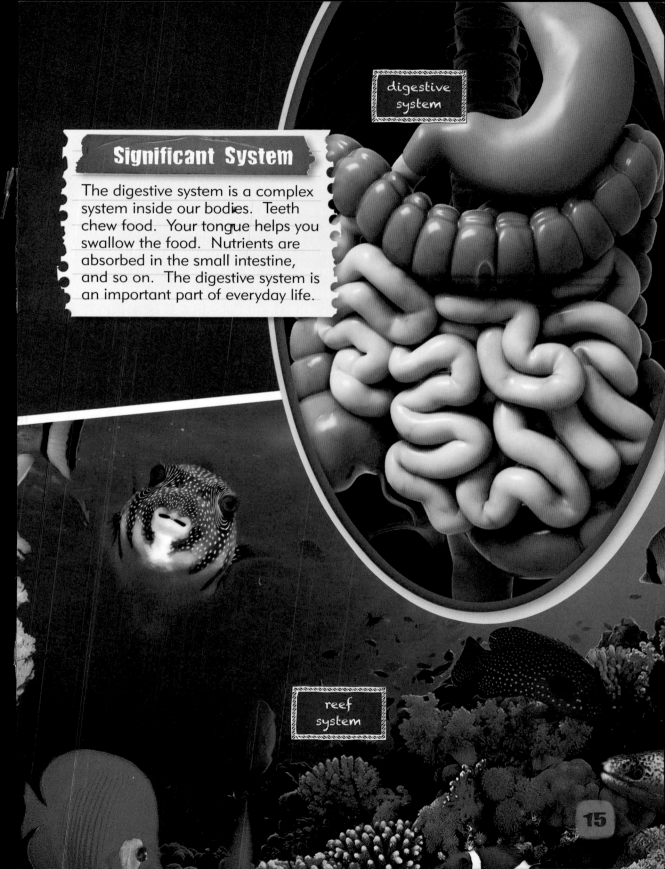

Significant System

The digestive system is a complex system inside our bodies. Teeth chew food. Your tongue helps you swallow the food. Nutrients are absorbed in the small intestine, and so on. The digestive system is an important part of everyday life.

reef
system

Say you have pure hydrogen and pure oxygen contained in a system. These two gases will react to create water.

To show reactions, scientists often use symbols to stand for chemicals. H_2O is the chemical symbol for water. It is made up of two hydrogen atoms and one oxygen atom. In this case, H stands for hydrogen. The 2 next to it means that there are two hydrogen atoms. The O stands for oxygen.

The equation below shows that if you start with two hydrogen atoms and one oxygen atom, they will combine to form one molecule of water, or H_2O. Even though the reaction ended with only one molecule, the mass was conserved because the number of atoms did not change. If you could somehow weigh the atoms before and after they combined, they would be the same. This is how the law of conservation of mass really works. It takes into account the mass of the atoms. Since atoms don't magically appear or disappear, their mass is conserved.

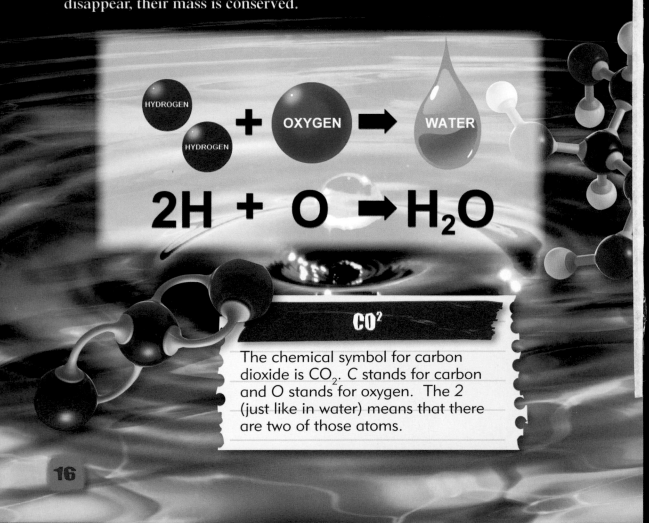

HYDROGEN

HYDROGEN

+   **OXYGEN**   ➡   **WATER**

$$2H + O \rightarrow H_2O$$

CO^2

The chemical symbol for carbon dioxide is CO_2. C stands for carbon and O stands for oxygen. The 2 (just like in water) means that there are two of those atoms.

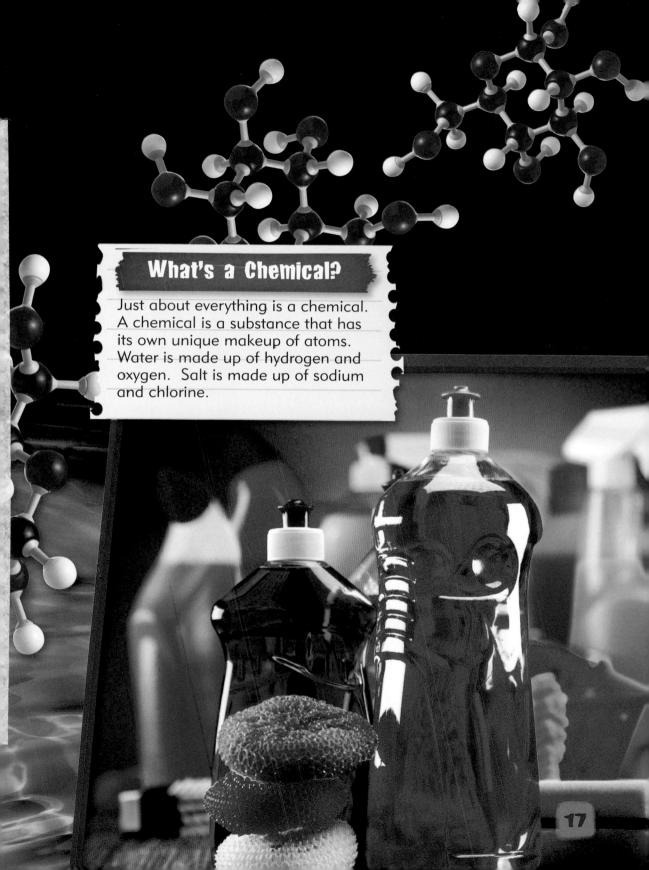

What's a Chemical?

Just about everything is a chemical. A chemical is a substance that has its own unique makeup of atoms. Water is made up of hydrogen and oxygen. Salt is made up of sodium and chlorine.

Energy Matters

Scientists study an object's mass and volume when an object changes, whether it's a piece of burning paper or a ripening banana. But Albert Einstein found that products come in one more form: energy. Like matter, energy can neither be created nor destroyed.

Einstein's theory of special relativity shows that mass and energy are related. This theory is summed up as $E = mc^2$. Each letter stands for a word. *E* stands for *energy*, *m* for *mass*, and *c* for the *speed of light*. The equation reads as *energy equals mass times the speed of light squared*. This means that the more mass an object has, the more energy it contains.

Einstein showed that matter could change into energy. And energy can become matter. In any reaction, the sum of the matter and the energy is constant. The two will always balance and add up to the same amount. So when scientists observe mass and volume to study changes in an object, in a way, they're actually measuring how the energy of an object has changed.

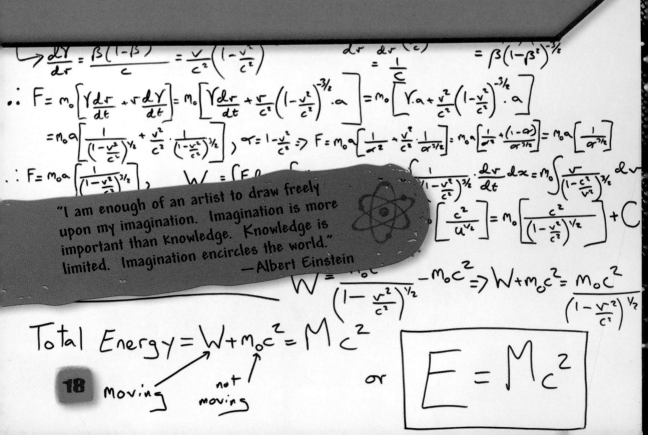

"I am enough of an artist to draw freely upon my imagination. Imagination is more important than knowledge. Knowledge is limited. Imagination encircles the world."
—Albert Einstein

$$\text{Total Energy} = W + m_o c^2 = Mc^2$$

Moving / not moving

or $\boxed{E = Mc^2}$

18

Making Science a Priority

Einstein was 26 years old when he came up with his theory of special relativity. He worked six days a week and had a wife and a son. Although he was busy, he made time for science.

History of the Law

We have come a long way in our understanding of atoms and the law of conservation of mass.

Our story starts in ancient Greece. A philosopher, Democritus, was the first to **hypothesize** that matter was made up of small particles. He observed that rocks can be broken down into small pieces of sand. So he thought that all matter can be broken down into smaller particles. He thought that at some point, you can break it down so small that you cannot break it any further. He called these particles *atomos*. This means "uncuttable." But his insight was largely ignored for hundreds of years.

In the early 1800s, John Dalton came up with several crucial ideas about atoms. Among other things, he stated that all matter is composed of tiny atoms. He also said that the same substances have the same types of atoms. And he said that when chemical reactions occur, atoms are rearranged.

Aristotle

Skepticism

Aristotle did not agree with Democritus. Since Aristotle was popular in the community during this time period, people ignored Democritus's theory.

John Dalton made it possible to identify elements based on their weights.

Democritus

A couple years earlier, French chemist Antoine Lavoisier (AN-twahn la-vwa-ZYEY) proved that matter could neither be created nor destroyed. Many people had thought that this may be true, but he was the first to experiment to prove this idea. He heated things in sealed glass containers. He found the containers had the same mass before and after they were heated. This was true even though the solid in the container changed. This led him to conclude that air contained mass, too. The mass in the system of the container was conserved. He and his wife, Marie-Anne, worked hard to get other scientists to accept his findings.

The work of these scientists and thinkers has guided us to our modern understanding of atoms and the conservation of mass. We now know that matter cannot be created or destroyed because atoms have mass. When chemical reactions take place, the atoms are simply rearranged. When we also consider Einstein's theory, we know that mass can be turned into energy. It doesn't disappear—it just changes form. This idea became a law.

Sodium burns with oxygen in a glass jar.

Today, Antoine Lavoisier is often referred to as the Father of Modern Chemistry.

Marie-Anne Lavoisier

Although history will tell you that Marie-Anne Lavoisier merely assisted her husband in his scientific studies, her work was just as important. She translated the research of other scientists for him, often pointing out their errors. She kept precise records and detailed drawings of the experiments they conducted together. She even made her husband publish the findings in a book that is still considered one of the best chemistry books ever written.

Words to Know

Scientists use many terms to talk about their ideas. But they may mean different things from what you're used to. For example, your friend might say that she has a theory about why she keeps losing her pens. What she really means is that she has a hunch or a guess. But scientists use terms such as theory much more carefully. A hypothesis, a theory, and a law are all different in science.

A hypothesis is a very educated guess. It is what a scientist believes to be true based on observations. A hypothesis must be testable. That way, scientists can conduct tests to decide whether they agree with the idea.

A theory is a scientific idea with strong evidence to support it. It has been tested over and over again and continues to hold up. A theory explains and makes predictions about the natural world.

A law summarizes many observations. But it does not explain why things happen. The law of conservation of mass does not explain why we can't make matter disappear. It just says that this is true. Scientists build on the law to explain why.

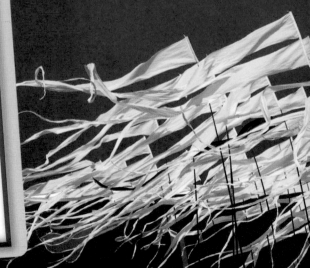

A

THEORY

OF THE

WINDS,

Shewing by a

New *HYPOTHESIS*,

THE

PHYSICAL CAUSES

Of all WINDS in General:

With the Solution of all the VARIETY and
PHÆNOMENA thereof,

As it was read to the ROYAL SOCIETY.

By *BERNARD ANNELY*.

LONDON:

Printed for JER. BATLEY, at the *Dove*
in *Pater-noster Row*. 1729.

Nothing Is Certain

A hypothesis, a theory, and a law can be disproven if new evidence arises. In science, nothing is ever "proven." All we can say is that there is very strong evidence to support an idea.

Copernicus

Disproving a Theory

In the past, people believed that Earth was the center of the universe. People thought that the sun revolved around Earth. However, this theory was disproven by Copernicus.

Mysterious Matter

Matter can neither be created nor destroyed. It's the law of conservation. But just because mass is conserved doesn't mean it always stays in the same form. It may be mixed or it may change state. It could even combine with other things in a chemical reaction. Regardless, the number of atoms will always remain the same. Einstein's theory of special relativity reveals that mass and energy are related. Matter can turn into energy and energy can become matter. So even when it looks like mass is not conserved, it really just changes.

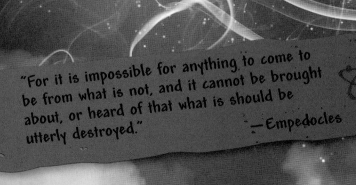

"For it is impossible for anything to come to be from what is not, and it cannot be brought about, or heard of that what is should be utterly destroyed."

—Empedocles

So the next time you express the fact that you're not a wizard who can make food appear out of thin air, just remember why. Our world is governed by rules and, yes, laws. But this is a good thing. You wouldn't want to live in a world in which nothing made sense. A random world would be a scary world. So be glad that nothing can come from nothing.

Think Like a Scientist

What happens to matter during a chemical reaction? Experiment and find out!

What to Get

- baking soda
- balloon
- funnel
- kitchen scale
- measuring cup
- measuring spoons
- vinegar
- water bottle

What to Do

1. Use the funnel to pour two teaspoons of baking soda into the balloon. Set the balloon aside.

2. Rinse the funnel, and then use it to pour $\frac{1}{4}$ cup of vinegar into the water bottle. Remove the funnel and set it aside.

3. Put the balloon around the mouth of the water bottle. Be careful not to pour the baking soda into the vinegar yet.

4. Place the water bottle with the balloon on the scale and record the weight.

5. Hold the balloon upright so that the baking soda falls into the bottle. What do you see? Place the bottle and balloon back onto the scale. Record the weight. What do you notice?

Glossary

atoms—the smallest particles of a substance that can exist by themselves

chemical changes—changes that result in new substances

environment—the natural world

hypothesis—an idea that is not proven and needs to be studied further

hypothesize—to suggest an idea to be tested

law—a scientific rule that always applies whenever certain conditions exist

mass—the amount of matter an object contains

matter—anything that has mass and takes up space

molecules—the smallest possible amounts of particular substances that have all the characteristics of the substances

physical change—a change that that does not form a new substance

product—the result of a chemical reaction, chemically distinct from the reactants

properties—special qualities or characteristics of something

reactant—a substance that changes when it is combined with another substance in a chemical reaction

system—a group of related parts that move or work together

theory—summarizes a hypothesis that has been supported with repeated testing

theory of special relativity—Einstein's theory that relates energy to mass

volume—amount of space that is filled by something

Index

Your Turn!

Sweet Conservation of Mass

Conduct your own experiment to observe conservation of mass. Gather ingredients to make cookies. Weigh and measure each ingredient separately. Once combined, weigh and measure the cookie dough mixture. How do the measurements and weights compare? Is this a physical change or a chemical change?